Crack-Whore

Piece of Shit

Fuck yeah

Fucker

Flip-a-Bitch

Jizz Mopper

Twat

壽

Thunder
Cunt

Cum
Dumpster

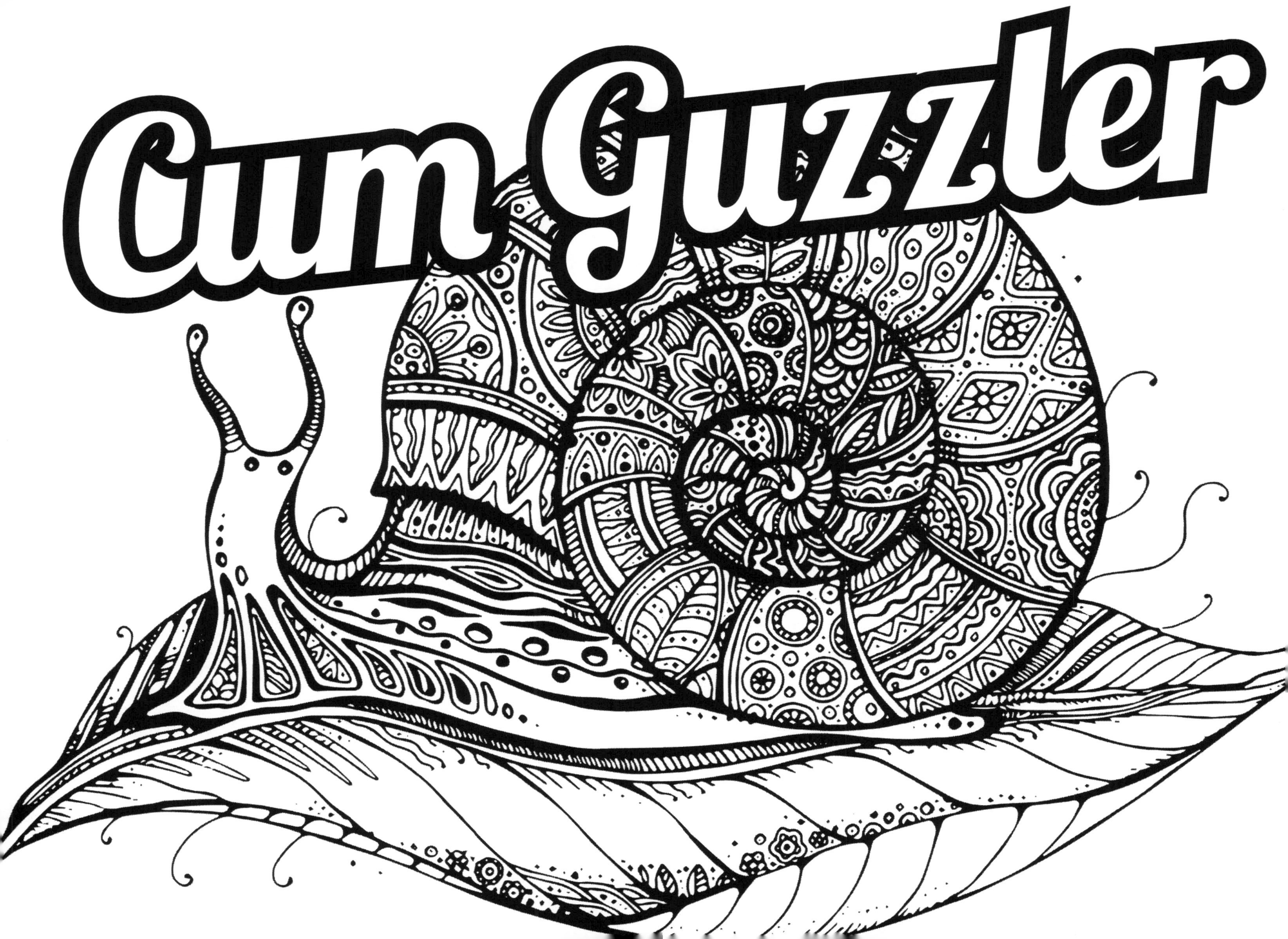
Cum Guzzler

Cockbag

Slutbag

Dickhead

Idiot

Fuck Off

Baggy
Vag

Moron

Shit-a-brick

Dipshit

Skank

Piss
Flaps

Twat
Waffle

Sugartits

Bastard

Fuck Boy

Cunt
Cake

Shitbag

Beaver Dam

Bitch

family

Asswipe

Asshat

Fuckballs

Asshole

Cunt

Wanker

Slut

Whore

Crap

Chode

Douche

Fucktard

Shitballs

Bollocks

Bitch

Damn

fuck

Bullshit

Shit

25027599R00057

Printed in Great Britain
by Amazon